SCOTLAND

SCOTLAND

HIGHLANDS, ISLANDS, LOCHS & LEGENDS

CLAUDIA MARTIN

amber
BOOKS

Published by
Amber Books Ltd
United House
North Road
London
N7 9DP
United Kingdom
www.amberbooks.co.uk
Instagram: @amberbooksltd
Facebook: www.facebook.com/amberbooks
Twitter: @amberbooks

Project Editor: Sarah Uttridge
Designer: Zoë Mellors
Picture Research: Terry Forshaw

ISBN: 978-1-78274-778-9

Printed in China

4 6 8 10 9 7 5 3 2

Contents

Introduction

Scotland's long history captures the imagination, with its intrepid saints, Viking warlords and battling clans. The country's wild landscapes are rich not just with birds and deer but with legend, from the myths of Fionn mac Cumhaill and his band of Fianna warriors to Bonnie Prince Charlie and the Highlanders who rallied behind him in 1745. Every one of Scotland's castles has a tale to tell, about a captive queen or the lord who gambled away his land. Even Scotland's wynds, streets and bridges have had stories and songs spun about them by the greatest of storytellers, from Robert Burns and Sir Walter Scott to Muriel Spark.

Yet Scotland has always been home to men and women who, while drawing strength from the traditions and stories of the past, have their thoughts fixed firmly on the future. It has been their groundbreaking ideas that forged Scotland into an industrial and intellectual powerhouse. Among them are the ambitious architects of Scotland's monuments ancient and modern; the myriad of engineers of canals and ships; the entrepreneurs who saw a chance and took it; and the craftspeople who made Paisley shawls and single malts.

ABOVE:
Isle of Mull, Inner Hebrides
Mull was known as 'Myl' to the Norse, 'Muile' to the Gaels and 'Malaeos' to the
Romans before them.
OPPOSITE:
Massed pipe bands, Dufftown, Moray
Pipe bands perform the Beating Retreat ceremony after the local Highland Games.

Edinburgh: Empress of the North

Scotland's capital has attracted many nicknames over its long history, from Edinburgh-born novelist Sir Walter Scott's emotive 'Empress of the North' to the more colloquial 'Auld Reekie', Scots for Old Smoky, because of the dark and smoke-wreathed Old Town. The town was recognized as the capital of Scotland from at least as long ago as the mid-14th century. Although the old Scottish parliament met in a number of locations, it came to rest in Edinburgh's Parliament Hall in the 17th century. In 1707, the parliaments of Scotland and England were merged, provoking riots across the city. In 1999, Edinburgh became home to the new devolved Scottish parliament. It was not until 2004 that the parliament had a permanent, and fittingly groundbreaking, purpose-built home, in Holyrood.

Edinburgh was at the heart of the Scottish Enlightenment of the 18th and early 19th centuries, a period when the great thinkers, mathematicians and scientists of Scotland spearheaded rapid advances. The halls of Edinburgh University and Medical School were walked by philosophers David Hume and Dugald Stewart, economist Adam Smith and physician Joseph Black. It was unsuprising that Edinburgh's scholars, along with its wealthy bankers, increasingly felt that the medieval city was overcrowded and unsanitary. The streets of the Old Town were adorned with monumental Neoclassical buildings, while from 1767 to 1850, the elegant New Town was laid out to the north. Since then, Edinburgh has continued to grow and develop, with cutting-edge new buildings and a world-famous arts festival, as befits its position as Empress of the North.

OPPOSITE:
Edinburgh Castle
There has been a castle on the outcrop known as Castle Rock since the reign of David I (1124–53) and probably earlier still. The oldest building within the fortifications is St Margaret's Chapel, built during David's reign in honour of his late mother, St Margaret of Scotland. Most buildings, however, date from after the Lang ('Long') Siege by English forces in 1571–73.

Edinburgh Castle and the Old Town
At the heart of the Old Town is Castle Rock, a volcanic plug formed when magma surged up the vent of a now extinct volcano some 350 million years ago. The Old Town still preserves some of its medieval street plan, with narrow closes and wynds leading off the main street, known as the Royal Mile, which descends a ridge from the crag. Many buildings here date from the 16th to 18th centuries.

LEFT:

Hogmanay Fireworks, Edinburgh Castle

The festival of Hogmanay, which is celebrated on 31 December, has its roots in mid-winter Norse festivals as well as the Gaelic festival of Samhain, when bonfires were lit and the boundary between the human world and the world of the spirits was at its weakest. All-night celebrations are held across Scotland, with the largest in Edinburgh, where the 400,000-strong crowd in 1996–7 broke the record for the largest New Year's party.

RIGHT:

Military Tattoo, Edinburgh Castle

The Military Tattoo takes place every August, as part of the Edinburgh Festival, the world's largest arts festival. A tattoo is a military performance, involving drills and marching bands of pipers and drummers, its name comes from the Dutch phrase *doe den tap toe* 'turn off the tap', a traditional signal by drummers or trumpeters to warn innkeepers near barracks to stop serving beer for the night. The first public Edinburgh Tattoo was held in 1949. Today, it attracts more than 200,000 spectators, plus a worldwide television audience.

Dugald Stewart Monument, Calton Hill

Edinburgh's craggy and hilly topography is the result of volcanism, faulting and glacial erosion. One of the city's most central green spaces is Calton Hill, site of several historic monuments, including the memorial to Dugald Stewart (1753–1828). Stewart was a mathematician and philosopher who did much to popularize the Scottish Enlightenment. His many influential pupils included novelist Sir Walter Scott and British prime minister Lord Palmerston. The monument, echoing the Corinthian architecture of ancient Greece, was designed in 1831 by Scottish architect William Henry Playfair.

LEFT:

Nelson Monument, Calton Hill

Designed in the form of an upturned telescope, a device much associated with Horatio Nelson (1758–1805), this tower was completed in 1815 to mark the naval commander's victory (and death) at the Battle of Trafalgar. At the top is a time ball, which is still raised then lowered at precisely 1 p.m. Its job was to signal to ships in Edinburgh's Leith port so they could set their chronometers.

Waverley Station

Located in a valley between the Old and New Towns, Edinburgh Waverley Railway Station was named after Sir Walter Scott's Waverley Novels, which were among the most widely read novels in Europe for many decades after the publication of the first book in 1814. The current main station building was built in 1868, on the site of three stations dating from the 1840s. The 1897 North Bridge runs above the tracks.

LEFT:

East Princes Street Gardens

The East Gardens, Edinburgh's most visited public park, were created in the 1770s, after construction on the New Town began, in 1767. They were originally a private garden for the residents of Princes Street. This area was under the waters of Nor Loch until the mid-18th century. The artificial lake was created as a defence by King James III in 1460, by building a dam along the line now occupied by North Bridge.

ABOVE:

National Gallery of Scotland

The Scottish National Gallery's Princes Street Gardens entrance, along with its underground education areas, was completed in 2004. The main building, designed by William Henry Playfair, responsible for so much of Edinburgh's Neoclassical cityscape, was completed in 1859. It holds notable works by Scottish painters such as James Guthrie, Henry Raeburn and Alexander Nasmyth, plus an exceptional collection of world art.

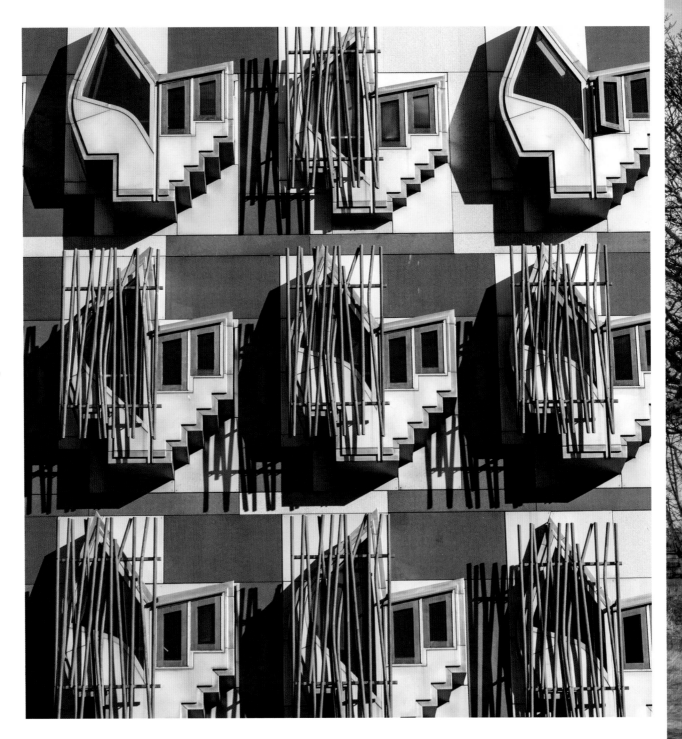

RIGHT:
Scottish Parliament Building, Holyrood
Opened in 2004, the Scottish Parliament Building was controversial during its construction because of spiralling costs and architect Enric Miralles's complex and groundbreaking design. The award-winning building continues to challenge, and engross, with its intensely crafted shapes and details that suggest many different meanings to every observer.

FAR RIGHT:
National Monument of Scotland, Calton Hill
Modelled on the Parthenon in Athens, this monument was designed by the ever busy William Henry Playfair, along with Charles Robert Cockerell. The construction of the memorial, honouring the Scottish dead of the Napoleonic Wars (1803–15), had to be left unfinished in 1829, due to lack of funds. Inevitably, this led to nicknames such as the 'National Disgrace'.

OPPOSITE AND LEFT:
St Giles' Cathedral
The present church dates from the 14th century, following a fire that destroyed most of the existing building in 1385. This was only a cathedral of the Church of Scotland in the technical sense (the seat of a bishop) in the 17th century. The 1911 Thistle Chapel (left) belongs to Scotland's highest chivalric order, the Order of the Thistle, consisting of the monarch (currently Elizabeth II) and 16 knights and ladies.

ABOVE:
Scott Monument, Princes Street Gardens
This 61-m (200-ft) high tower honours one of Scotland's most beloved novelists, Sir Walter Scott (1771–1832). Completed in 1844, the monument features statues of Scott and his dog, plus 92 other figures, including characters from Scotts' romantic and gripping historical novels *Waverley*, *Ivanhoe*, *Rob Roy* and many others.

City Chambers, Royal Mile
Now home to Edinburgh City Council, this building was opened as the Royal Exchange, a centre of commerce for merchants, in 1760. The core of the building was designed by Scottish architect John Adam, older brother of the more famous Robert Adam and son of the prolific William. The building was never popular with merchants, who preferred to do business in local taverns or simply outdoors at the site of the nearby Mercat Cross, so the building was taken over by the council in 1811.

Royal Mile
The Royal Mile runs for almost exactly a mile between Edinburgh Castle and the Palace of Holyroodhouse, both home to Scottish royalty during their long history. The Royal Mile is not officially so named, taking on the title only in the 20th century. From east to west, the true street names are Abbey Strand, Canongate, High Street (pictured), Lawnmarket and Castlehill.

LEFT:

Old College, University of Edinburgh, Nicholson Street
Originally named the New College, this building was constructed between 1789 and 1831 to designs by the great Neoclassical Scottish architect Robert Adam (1728–92), carried through after his death by the ubiquitous William Henry Playfair. The dome, proposed by Adam, was added in 1887 by one of the other great men of Scottish public architecture, Sir Robert Rowand Anderson.

RIGHT:

Telephone boxes, Royal Mile
The iconic red phone box, the 'K2', once found throughout the United Kingdom and its former or current British colonies, was designed by Sir Giles Gilbert Scott in 1924. It is in a Classical style, with a domed roof, and in red to make it easy to spot. Most red boxes were replaced from the 1980s with more utilitarian, and wheelchair-accessible, designs. Still beloved by the public, the boxes were kept in heritage areas and some rural locations. Some now house cash machines.

**The Royal Mile
Tavern, Royal Mile**

This traditional pub is one
of more than a dozen pubs
on the Royal Mile. In 2007, a
survey found that Edinburgh
may be the city in the United
Kingdom with more pubs
per square mile than any
other, with more than 700
in total. However, this is a
hottly contested title. Another
contested title is for the city's
oldest pub. The winner may
be the Sheep Heid Inn, near
Holyrood Park, which may
have been serving since 1360.

**Statue of David Hume,
Royal Mile**

This statue of the Scottish
philosopher David Hume
(1711–76) was completed
in 1995, at 1.5 times actual
size. Ironically for this great
rational thinker of the Scottish
Enlightenment who staunchly
opposed superstition, the
statue has become the subject
of a superstition. It is said that
rubbing Hume's protruding
toe will bring good luck. The
strength of the superstition is
proved by the toe's shininess.

LEFT:

Palace of Holyroodhouse

With the exception of the 16th-century northwest tower (pictured at far left), this palace was largely constructed from 1671 to 1678 for King Charles II of England, Scotland and Ireland. The southwest tower was designed to match its twin, with the rest of the building conceived in Neoclassical Palladian style by the aristocratic gentleman-architect Sir William Bruce. The palace is still the official residence of the British monarch in Scotland. Queen Elizabeth II spends one week here every summer.

RIGHT:

The Quadrangle, Holyroodhouse

Each of the three floors of this colonnaded internal courtyard sports columns from one of the three Classical Greek orders of architecture. The simplest Doric order is used for the ground floor, home to the palace's services; the Ionic order is used on the first floor, where the state apartments are found; and the elaborate Corinthian order is used for the second floor, home to the royal apartments.

Kilts

The first records of kilt-wearing date back to the 16th century, when men were wearing 'great kilts', full length, belted garments whose upper half was worn as a cloak. Shorter 'walking kilts', similar to the modern kilt, were worn from the late 17th or early 18th century. 'Kilt' means 'to tuck up the clothes'. The garment probably grew from woollen cloaks, known as plaids, which were worn over tunics. Kilts and tartans, as symbols of the power of Highland clans, were banned by the government of George II in the Dress Act of 1746.

Tartans

Tartans, which are checked patterns in woven cloth, were originally associated with districts. The different patterns were the result of the dyes available to weavers and the tastes of their local buyers. When the Dress Act was repealed in 1782, tartans and kilts had stopped being ordinary Highland dress, but they were adopted again as a symbol of Scottish identity. It was only in the mid-19th century that particular patterns came to be adopted by clans and institutions that wanted to express their kinship with Scottish history.

Twill

Tartan is traditionally woven from wool in the twill style. In this method, threads dyed in different colours are woven as warp and weft at right angles to each other. The weft is woven two over, then two under the warp, but with an offset, or 'step', at each pass, which forms diagonal lines where different colours cross. This distinctive diagonal pattern is known as the wale. Here the colours appear to blend with each other, forming new shades. The blocks of colour, creating a basic 'tile' known as a sett, repeat both vertically and horizontally.

ABOVE:

Knitwear

By the 16th and 17th centuries, knitting was a key cottage industry in Scotland, particularly in the islands. The Fair Isle technique, which uses a palette of five colours to create traditional patterns, found widespread popularity after such sweaters were worn by the future Edward VIII in the 1920s. Other popular styles include the diamond-patterned Argyle, popularized by Pringle of Scotland, which was established in the Scottish Borders in 1815.

BELOW:

Circus Lane, New Town

Edinburgh's New Town was built between 1767 and 1850, in a series of planned extensions that filled fields and incorporated existing villages to the north of the cramped Old Town. The village of Stockbridge (pictured) was developed from around 1813. St Stephen's Church was designed by William Henry Playfair in 1827. It boasts the longest clock pendulum in Europe, swinging in its 49m (162ft) tower.

RIGHT:

The Vennel, Old Town

A vennel, from the Old French for alley or lane (related to the English word 'funnel'), is a narrow public way between buildings. The Vennel steps, leading down to Grassmarket and with views of the Castle, were seen in the 1969 film *The Prime of Miss Jean Brodie*, starring Maggie Smith as an unshackled teacher at an Edinburgh girls' school, based on the book by Muriel Spark.

LEFT:

Tolbooth Tavern, Canongate

The Tolbooth Tavern is part of the Canongate Tolbooth, built around 1591 as the courthouse, prison and council rooms of Canongate, which was then a separate burgh outside the town walls. Canongate was bought by Edinburgh in 1636. The pub is said to have a poltergeist, guilty of knocking pints off tables, although there may be other explanations for the phenomenon.

ABOVE:

Statue of Greyfriars Bobby, Candlemaker Row

This statue commemorates the Skye terrier who became famous for guarding the grave of his owner, John Gray, in nearby Greyfriars Kirkyard for 14 years, until his own death in 1872. The dog was buried just inside the gate of Greyfriars Kirkyard, not far from his owner. Some have cast doubt on the story, suggesting Bobby may just have been a stray.

New Calton Burial Ground, Regent Road

On the southeastern slope of Calton Hill, this cemetery was opened in 1817 as an overspill from nearby Old Calton Burial Ground. The Watch Tower (pictured at centre back) was built to protect against grave robbing. Despite its 5m (16ft) diameter, it was a home until 1955. The family cultivated a kitchen garden in adjacent empty plots.

Old Calton Burial Ground, Calton Hill

Opened in 1718, this city-managed cemetery is home to the graves of philospher David Hume, whisky distiller John Haig, mathematician John Playfair and painter David Allan. The obelisk is the Political Martyrs' Monument in honour of the five men, led by Thomas Muir, who campaigned for universal suffrage and in 1793 were deported to Australia for their efforts.

RIGHT:

Canongate Kirkyard
This churchyard, surrounding
Canongate Kirk, was used for
burials from 1688 until 1963,
when architect Robert Hurd
was laid to rest here, after the
ground's official closure. Hurd
was given this honour because
of his work in surrounding
Canongate. The most famous
burial is arguably Scottish
economist Adam Smith
(1723–90), who laid the
foundations for the theory of
free market trade in his *The
Wealth of Nations* (1776).

FAR RIGHT:

**Canongate Kirk and
Salisbury Crags**
Seen from Calton Hill,
Canongate Kirk is pictured
with a backdrop of Salisbury
Crags. The church, completed
in 1691, serves the parish
of Canongate, including
Holyroodhouse. The
wedding of Elizabeth II's
granddaughter Zara Tindall
(née Phillips) was held here
in 2011.

Salisbury Crags and Arthur's Seat

The Salisbury Crags are steep cliffs of erosion-resistant dolerite and columnar basalt, on top of a spur of the hill known as Arthur's Seat (pictured directly below). At 251m (823ft), Arthur's Seat is the highest hill in Holyrood Park, just to the east of the city centre. The name may have arisen from legends of King Arthur or may have developed from a Scottish Gaelic phrase such as Àrd-thir Suidhe, meaning 'place on high ground'.

BELOW:

Newhaven Harbour

Now a suburb of Edinburgh, Newhaven was once a fishing village famous for its oysters and, from 1504, a major centre for shipbuilding. It was James IV's custom-built port, designed to have enough space to construct his mammoth warship, the 73-m (240-ft) long *Michael*. When launched in 1511, she was the longest ship afloat. The lighthouse at the current harbour entrance was built in 1869.

OPPOSITE:

Leith

Just to the east of Newhaven, the village of Leith had grown into a burgh by 1833 and, despite a referendum in which 86 per cent of Leith's inhabitants voted against, was merged with Edinburgh in 1920. The Signal Tower (pictured at the far left), built in 1686, was originally a windmill. In 1805, the sails were removed, crenellations were added and the roof began to display flags to signal to ships the depth of water at the harbour bar.

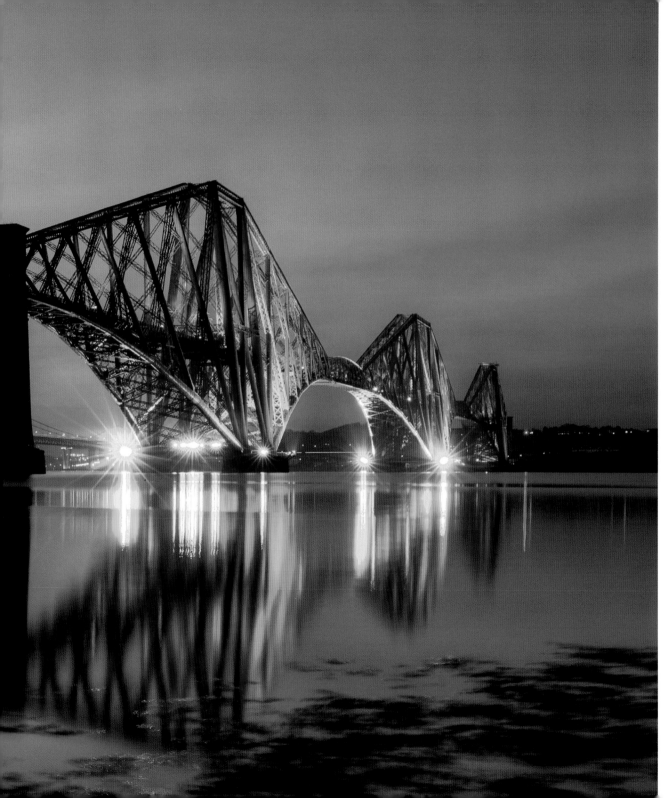

LEFT:

Forth Bridge, Firth of Forth, Edinburgh–Fife
This railway bridge, 14km (9 miles) west of Edinburgh, boasted the longest cantilever bridge span in the world when it opened in 1890. Designed by civil engineers Sir John Fowler and Sir Benjamin Baker, the bridge is 2467m (8094ft) long and was the first major structure in Britain to be constructed from steel.

ABOVE:

Queensferry Crossing, Firth of Forth
Fifty-three years after opening the Forth Road Bridge (pictured in the background of the photo to the left), Queen Elizabeth II opened this replacement bridge in 2017, just to the west. The cable-stayed bridge carries the M90 motorway, while the old suspension bridge carries only buses, bikes and pedestrians.

The Highlands: Mountains and Lochs

In geographical terms, the Highlands are the mountainous region to the north of the Highland Boundary Fault, which crosses Scotland from the Isle of Arran on the west coast to Stonehaven on the east. The rocks to the north of this fault were uplifted during the Caledonian orogeny, a period of continental collision and mountain-building that took place around 490–380 million years ago. Ice ages over the last 2.5 million years, as well as swift mountain streams, did their work on this landscape, scouring glens and lochs. All of Scotland's 282 Munros are in the Highlands. A Munro is a Scottish peak taller than 914.4m (3000ft), named after Sir Hugh Munro (1856–1919), who first compiled the list. 'Munro-bagging', or climbing every mountain on the list, is a popular challenge, completed by 6000 people and counting.

No less than their distinct topography, the Highlands have their own cultural character. Historically, this was the Scottish Gaelic-speaking region, while the Lowlanders spoke Scots. Scottish Gaelic is a Celtic language, like Irish, Welsh, Breton, Cornish and Manx. Scots is a sister language or dialect of English. The Highlands were also the stronghold of the clans, kinship groupings that have their origins in medieval warlords and their bands. These chiefs were often of Gaelic or Norse descent but may also have been Norman, Anglo-Norman or Flemish. During the wars of independence between Scotland and England in the late 13th and early 14th centuries, the kings of Scotland, particularly Robert the Bruce, harnessed and formalized the power of the clans. Later, it was among the Highland clans that the 18th-century Jacobite Risings began.

OPPOSITE:
Praying Hands of Mary, Glen Lyon, Perth and Kinross
At 54-km (34-miles) long, Glen Lyon, in the southern Highlands, is the longest enclosed glen in Scotland. The word 'glen' comes from the Scottish Gaelic (and Irish) *gleann*, meaning a long, deep valley. The Praying Hands are a natural formation, also known as Fionn's Rock after a legend that tells how the rock was split by the hero Fionn mac Cumhaill's arrow.

LEFT:

Glenfinnan Viaduct, Inverness-shire

This 1901 single-track railway bridge crosses the River Finnan near Loch Shiel. Made from unreinforced concrete, the viaduct has 21 15-m (50-ft) semicircular spans. The line is used by trains between Glasgow and Mallaig, plus, in the summer, the *Jacobite* steam train (pictured). The viaduct has featured in many movies and TV shows, including the *Harry Potter* films and 1969's *Ring of Bright Water*.

TOP RIGHT:

Neptune's Staircase, Caledonian Canal, Lochaber

Built by Scottish civil engineer Thomas Telford between 1803 and 1822, this system of eight locks is Britain's longest staircase lock. The system lifts boats a total of 19.5m (64ft), taking a minimum of 90 minutes to pass through.

BOTTOM RIGHT:

Caledonian Canal and Ben Nevis at Corpach, Lochaber

Telford's Caledonian Canal is 60 miles (97 km) long, connecting the west coast at Corpach with the east coast at Inverness. Two-thirds of the canal are formed by natural waterways: Loch Dochfour, Loch Ness, Loch Oich and Loch Lochy. Ben Nevis, the United Kingdom's tallest mountain at 1345m (4411ft), is pictured at the right of the photograph.

Three Sisters of Glen Coe, Lochaber
The Three Sisters are steep-sided ridges of Bidean nam Bian, which at 1149m (3771ft) tall is number 24 on the Scottish Mountaineering Club's list of Munros. The ridges extend north into Glen Coe, a valley formed 420 million years ago by the collapse of a supervolcano, then shaped by ice age glaciers.

LEFT:

Torren Lochan, Glen Coe

As remembered by local place names, Glen Coe is said to have been home to the warrior giants of Fionn mac Cumhaill. Fionn's son Ossian was born in a cave here, known as Ossian's Cave. Fittingly, this *lochan* (small lake) in the glen was the location for Hagrid's hut in the *Prisoner of Azkaban*. The glen is also rightly infamous as the site of the 1692 Massacre of Glencoe, when 38 MacDonalds were betrayed and killed by government forces.

ABOVE:

Buachaille Etive Mòr, Glen Etive, Lochaber

At the entrance to Glen Coe, at the head of Glen Etive, is the 1021m (3350ft) Buachaille Etive Mòr (Herdsman of Etive), number 109 on the list of Munros. The cottage at its foot, Lagangarbh Hut, offers accommodation for climbers. The mountain has been a location in films ranging from the 1998 Bollywood smash-hit *Kuch Kuch Hota Hai* (*Something... Something Happens*) to the 2012 James Bond *Skyfall*.

TOP LEFT:

Loch Rannoch Folly, Perth and Kinross

This *crannog* (artificial island) lies in Loch Rannoch, a freshwater lake. *Crannogs* were built from wooden piles, and sometimes stone, from the Iron Age to as late as the 17th century, with around 500 in Scotland and 1,200 in Ireland. The *crannog*'s folly, probably built by a local baron, dates back to the 19th century.

BOTTOM LEFT:

The Wee Hoose, Loch Shin, Sutherland

The local story goes that this tiny house was built by a 19th-century poacher named Jock Broon, awarded land by the laird for his whisky-distilling skills. Sadly, Jock died after shooting himself in the foot. An alternative to this story is that the house was built a few years ago for the annual Lairg Gala, a local community festival. The choice of which story to believe is yours.

RIGHT:

Loch Shiel, Lochaber

A freshwater loch, Shiel was formed about 10,000 years ago, when a retreating glacier deposited rocks, blocking the mouth of a sea loch. The Glenfinnan Monument (pictured) at the lake's head was erected in 1815 in memory of the clansmen who died in the Jacobite Rising of 1745. It was here that Bonnie Prince Charlie (1720–88) raised the Stewart standard flag.

Loch Cluanie, Lochaber
Loch Cluanie was created in 1957 by the building of the Cluanie Dam. The surrounding remnants of Caledonian pinewood are home to red deer, red squirrels, black grouse and ptarmigan. The Victorian Cluanie Lodge (pictured) overlooks the lake at the southwestern end.

ABOVE:

Mallaig Harbour, Lochaber

The busy fishing port of Mallaig was founded only in 1840, when the local landowner, Lord Lovat, encouraged his crofters to move to the coast, away from the densely populated land between Lochs Morar and Nevis, and become fishermen. How willing they were to do so is unknown, but Mallaig was soon thriving, landing large quantities of herring and becoming famous for its traditionally smoked kippers.

RIGHT:

Arisaig, Lochaber

The west-coast area around the small village of Arisaig changed hands many times over the centuries. It was part of the Norwegian Kingdom of the Isles from around the 9th century to the late 11th century, when it was claimed by Scotland. In the 12th century, the area came under the control of Somerled, a Norse-Gaelic warlord, before passing back to Norway. From 1266, it once more belonged to the Scottish crown.

**Plockton,
Ross and Cromarty**
Plockton was built on a
ploc (Gaelic for 'bump') of
the peninsula of Lochalsh,
in a sheltered inlet of Loch
Carron. The village's location
gives it a mild climate and
allows many New Zealand
cabbage palms to grow, first
introduced in the 1960s.
Plockton was the location for
the 1990s television detective
series *Hamish Macbeth*,
starring Robert Carlisle.

Dornie, Ross and Cromarty
Before the building of a
bridge, the ferry from Dornie
across Loch Long, gave rise
to the traditional bagpipe
tune 'Dornie Ferry'. This is a
strathspey, a dance in 4/4 time,
played slightly slower than
a reel, with an exaggerated
syncopated rhythm.

Avoch, Ross and Cromarty
This fishing village lies on
the Black Isle on the Moray
Firth, on Scotland's east
coast. Despite its name, the
Black Isle is a peninsula.
The fisherfolk of Avoch and
Cromarty were speakers of
their own dialect of North
Northern Scots, itself a dialect
of Lowland Scots. It became
extinct on the death of Bobby
Hogg in 2012.

Kilchurn Castle, Loch Awe, Argyll and Bute
Built by the Campbells of Glenorchy, a powerful branch of Clan Campbell, in around 1450, this castle was abandoned after a lightning strike in 1760. When first built, the castle was on a tiny island, accessed by a low causeway. In the early 19th century, drainage work on freshwater Loch Awe lowered the water level, since when the castle has been on a promontory.

TOP LEFT:

Castle Stalker, Loch Laich, Argyll and Bute

Castle Stalker is a fortified tower house built around 1440 by Clan Stewart of Appin. In around 1620, a drunken bet resulted in the castle passing into the ownership of Clan Campbell, in return for an eight-oared wherry. Stalker found fame as the Castle of Aaaaarrrrrggghhh in 1975's *Monty Python and the Holy Grail.*

BOTTOM LEFT:

Ardvreck Castle, Loch Assynt, Sutherland

Built around 1590 by Clan MacLeod, this castle was captured by Clan MacKenzie in 1672. They used some of its stones to build a more modern house nearby. The ruins of the large three-storey stronghold consist of parts of a tower and defensive wall.

RIGHT:

Eilean Donan Castle, Ross and Cromarty

Situated on the tidal island ('*eilean*') of Donan, this castle was built in the 20th century to the ground plan of a 13th-century castle destroyed by the Royal Navy in 1719, following a Jacobite Rising. The rebuilding, between 1919 and 1932, was more a romantic reimagining of a medieval castle than a faithful reconstruction.

Inveraray Castle, Argyll and Bute

This Gothic Revival-style castle was begun in 1746 for the Dukes of Argyll, replacing a 15th-century castle. In the 1770s, the nearby village of Inveraray was moved to improve views from the castle, gaining handsome buildings designed by John Adam, brother to Robert and James and son to William. The 13th Duke of Argyll, captain of Scotland's elephant polo team, lives in the castle with his family for part of the year.

Balmoral Castle, Aberdeenshire

Balmoral has been the private property of the royal family since 1852, when the estate and its old castle were bought by Prince Albert, because its hilly landscape reminded him of his homeland of Thuringia, Germany. A new and larger castle was soon designed by Scottish architect William Smith, in Scottish Baronial style, harking back to medieval tower houses but with the addition of grand Renaissance elements.

LEFT:

**An Teallach,
Ross and Cromarty**

An Teallach (meaning 'The
Forge' in Scottish Gaelic) is
a ridge with 14 peaks, the
tallest of which, Bidein a'
Ghlas Thuill, rises to 1062m
(3484ft) and is number 72 on
the list of Munros. The road
that winds to the mountain
from Dundonnell, called
'Desolation Road', was built
to give employment to crofters
during the famine of 1846–7.
They were paid in rations.

ABOVE:

**Scots pine, Lairig Ghru Pass,
Cairngorms, Aberdeenshire**

The Scots pine was a key
species of the Caledonian
pinewoods that once covered
much of Scotland, growing
on thin, infertile soils. The
pinewoods have been slowly
cleared since Neolithic times,
leaving only 35 remnants that
cover 180 sq km (69 sq miles).
The Lairig Ghru is a 835-m
(2740-ft) high pass through
the Cairngorm mountains of
the eastern Highlands.

**Cairngorms National Park,
Aberdeenshire**
Carn Eilrig (in the foreground
of the photo above) rises
to 742m (2434ft). At 1245m
(4085ft), Cairn Gorm itself,
which means 'Blue or Green
Hill' in Scottish Gaelic, is not
the highest mountain in the
Cairngorm range, the honour
of which falls to 1309-m
(4295-ft) Ben Macdui.
There are more than 20
lochs within the Cairngorms
National Park, the largest
national park in the British
Isles. One of the most easily
accessible is Loch Garten
(pictured left), home to a
large breeding population
of ospreys.

Waterfall at Glen Feshie, Cairngorms

It was in Glen Feshie that Edwin Landseer painted his *The Monarch of the Glen*, depicting a red deer stag, in 1851. The upper reaches of Glen Feshie are covered by Caledonian pinewoods. To preserve these remnants, the deer population is now being managed, to prevent overgrazing on seedlings of Scotch pine, birch, juniper, willow and rowan.

Goldfinch, Cairngorms

European goldfinches are a common sight in the Cairngorms, particularly in summer. Due to the range of habitats in the park, it is host to one-quarter of the United Kingdom's threatened species. Visitors may be lucky enough to see birds such as golden eagles, ospreys, capercaillie, ptarmigan, dotterel and crested tits, and mammals from red squirrels to wildcats and mountain hares.

LEFT:

**Red deer stag,
Loch Arkaig, Lochaber**

Red deer are the United Kingdom's largest native mammals. Only the stags grow antlers, which are shed at the end of winter and regrown in spring, at up to 2.5 cm (1 in) per day. Conservation and reintroduction attempts have seen the numbers of red deer grow in the United Kingdom, with substantial populations in Scotland, some hybridized with the introduced sika deer.

BELOW:

**Reindeer,
Ben Macdui, Cairngorms**

The United Kingdom's only herd of wild reindeer lives in the Cairngorms National Park and the Glenlivet Estate. There are 150 animals in the herd, which was introduced from Sweden in 1952. Before this date, it is believed that the British Isles' last wild reindeer had died out around 800 years ago. The tundra-like conditions on these mountain peaks allow the herd to thrive.

Loch Arklet, Stirling
Lying between Lochs Lomond and Katrine, in the Loch Lomond and the Trossachs National Park, is the rugged and remote Loch Arklet. In the background, the Arrochar Alps boast 5 of the park's 21 Munros. The most southerly Munro, the 974m (3196-ft) Ben Lomond, lies within the park boundaries.

LEFT:

Loch an Eilein, Badenoch and Strathspey

This freshwater lake, which freezes over in winter, lies in Rothiemurchus Forest, a pocket of Caledonian pinewood. The loch's name translates from Scottish Gaelic as 'Lake of the Island'. A path along one side of the loch is known as Robbers Way, after the cattle rustlers who used it, including – so the story goes – Rob Roy MacGregor (1671–1734). Rob Roy took part in the Jacobite Risings, later being outlawed for his cattle rustling and protection racket.

RIGHT:

Loch Eilt, Lochaber

Loch Eilt has a number of small Scots pine-clad islands, including Eilean na Moine, which was shot as the location for Dumbledore's grave in the *Harry Potter* movies, then digitally placed on Loch Arkaig. Behind the lake is Rois-bheinn, one of the most prominent hills in the British Isles because of the deep pass formed by the loch, although the peak reaches only 882m (2894ft).

ABOVE:

Stac Pollaidh, Ross and Cromarty

The mountain of Stac Pollaidh is crowned by a sandstone crest known as a nunatak, left exposed and uneroded as glaciers carved the lower slopes during the last ice age. The mountain's name, which has its roots in both Scottish Gaelic and Norse, roughly translates as 'Pinnacle of the River Pool'. The summit, which is a relatively easy scramble, offers views over the Inverpolly Forest and the Atlantic Ocean.

RIGHT:

Loch Katrine, Stirling

This 13-km (8-mile) long loch has provided drinking water to Glasgow since 1859, via the Milngavie water treatment works and two 56km (32 mile) aqueducts. To protect water quality, the loch's tourist steamboat, the SS *Sir Walter Scott*, is now powered by biofuel. In operation since 1900, the boat honours the author of the 1810 poem *Lady of the Lake* and 1818 novel *Rob Roy*, which are both set around Loch Katrine.

LEFT:

Ardnamurchan Lighthouse, Lochaber

This unusual lighthouse, with detailing inspired by the architecture of ancient Egypt, was designed by Alan Stevenson in 1849. Stevenson, who built 14 lighthouses, was the uncle of novelist Robert Louis Stevenson. Alan's father Robert, brothers Thomas and David, and nephews Charles and David Alan were also prolific lighthouse designers, being responsible for nearly all Scotland's lighthouses for 125 years.

ABOVE:

Cromarty Lighthouse, Ross and Cromarty

Another of Alan Stevenson's works was Cromarty Lighthouse, completed in 1846 to guide ships in from the Moray Firth to the Cromarty Firth. The lighthouse was automated in 1985, then decommissioned in 2005. The buildings are now used for marine research by the University of Aberdeen's School of Biological Sciences. The Cromarty coast is one of the best places in Europe to see bottlenose dolphins playing close to the shore.

83

TOP LEFT:

Loch Linnhe, Lochaber

Loch Linnhe is the only sea loch in the line of lochs, including Loch Ness and Loch Lochy (right), along the geological fault known as the Great Glen. This cleft runs from near Oban on the west coast to near Inverness on the east coast.

BOTTOM LEFT:

Loch Leven, Perth and Kinross

Mary, Queen of Scots was imprisoned on an island on this freshwater lake from 1567–8, before escaping with the help of her gaolers. In 1831, a sceptre with the words 'Mary, Queen of Scots' is said to have been uncovered here when the lake's water level dropped during the canalization of the River Leven.

RIGHT:

Loch Lochy, Lochaber

Just to the southwest of Loch Ness, Loch Lochy is also credited with being home to legendary creatures. According to local lore, the River Horse emerges from the lake to feed on the banks, overturn boats and entice away mares. Another creature is the more harmless River Bull, which emerges from the lake to feed with the cows.

Loch Maree, Ross and Cromarty
Towering above the southeast shores of Loch Maree is the mountain of Slioch, reaching a height of 981m (3219ft) and taking 170 on the list of Munros. The mountain takes its name from the Scottish Gaelic word for spear ('*sleagh*'). The mountain is known for its feral goats, while 12 species of dragonflies, including the northern emerald and azure hawker, have been noted on the shores and islands of the loch.

Luss Pier, Loch Lomond, Argyll and Bute
The pier at Luss is a popular starting point for boat trips on Loch Lomond, which – at 71 sq km (27.5 sq miles) – is the largest inland body of water by surface area in Great Britain. The lake's biggest island, Inchmurrin, is the largest freshwater island in the British Isles. The loch was immortalized in the traditional song 'The Bonnie Banks o' Loch Lomond', first published in 1841 but probably rooted in the Jacobite Risings.

Loch Ness, Inverness-shire
This 37-km (23-mile) long freshwater lake is the largest by volume in the British Isles, because of its great depth of 230m (755ft). Some believe those depths hide one of the world's most famous cryptids, the Loch Ness Monster. 'Nessie' was first brought to the world's attention in 1933, when George Spicer and his wife saw 'a most extraordinary form of animal' lurch into the lake. Further apparent sightings, including hoaxes such as the famous *Daily Mail*-published photograph of 1934, have suggested a large, long-necked creature. Some think that Nessie is no more than wishful thinking, while others suspect a misidentified eel, wels catfish or even seismic gas released from the Great Glen Fault below.

The Islands: Ancient Worlds

Scotland has 790 islands, most of them in the archipelagoes of the Inner and Outer Hebrides, off the west coast, and the Orkney and Shetland Islands to the north. The Hebrides have been Scottish territory since 1266, when Magnus VI of Norway signed them over to Alexander III of Scotland. The Orkney and Shetland Islands remained under Norwegian rule until 1472. The names of the islands reflect their history, with most of the Hebrides having names with Scottish Gaelic roots, while many of the Northern Isles have names derived from Old Norse. Yet the islands were inhabited long before colonization by the Gaels or Vikings, as vouchsafed by some of the world's most evocative Neolithic sites, from Orkney's Skara Brae to Lewis's stone circles.

Eighty-nine of Scotland's offshore islands are permanently inhabited. Some of today's uninhabited islands were peopled within living memory, including the most westerly islands in the Hebrides, St Kilda, which were lived on until 1930, when the islanders asked to be rehoused on the mainland. Depopulation began during the 18th and 19th centuries because of poverty, famine and the Highland Clearances, when landowners enclosed common lands to rear sheep. However, between the 2001 and 2011 censuses, the population of the Scottish islands grew from 99,739 to 103,702. Today, the islands are thriving, in part because of their inhabitants' determination not only to preserve but to give new life to their traditions, whether Gaelic, Norse or far older.

OPPOSITE:
Red deer stag, Blue Pool, Glen Rosa, Arran
Glen Rosa, with its tumbling river, cuts west of Brodick, Arran's largest town. Red deer herds can be found on these hillsides, along with breeding hen harriers, which are critically endangered in the United Kingdom. Other endangered species on the island include three species of tree endemic to Arran: the Arran, cut-leaved and Catacol whitebeams.

Cabbage palms, near Lamlash, Arran

The New Zealand cabbage palm, which despite its appearance is not a true palm tree, was imported from the 19th century. This monocot can survive in a cool maritime climate as far north as Masfjorden, Norway, as long as it is protected from the iciest winds and frost. Lamlash, in a sheltered bay on Arran's east coast, is renowned for the many seals that can be spotted sunning themselves close to shore.

Goat Fell, Arran

At 874m (2,867ft), the pyramidal Goat Fell is the highest mountain on Arran. The peak's name may come from the Norse for 'goat' (*geita*), thanks to its mountain goats, or from the Gaelic for 'mountain wind' (*gaoth*). The scramble up to the summit is considered one of the loveliest in Scotland, offering views to the Isle of Jura, Ben Lomond on the mainland, and the coast of Ireland.

LEFT:

Brodick Bay, Arran

Fishing, along with farming, was once Arran's key industry. Today, while some islanders are still engaged in small-scale sustainable fishing, key industries for the island's population of 4600 are tourism, forestry and brewing. Some of the waters around the island are a No Take Zone to protect marine life.

RIGHT:

The Twelve Apostles, Catacol, Arran

Facing the sea in the small village of Catacol are the fishermen's cottages known as the Twelve Apostles. Each has a different upper-storey window so that, when the men were fishing in the Firth of Clyde, their families could light a candle in the window and the men would know which house was signalling.

Machrie Moor, Arran

Machrie Moor is home to seven stone circles, plus chambered cairns and individual standing stones. The circles were erected around 500 BC, but are on top of timber circles dated to around 2000 BC. Stone circle 3 (pictured) originally had nine stones, of which only one, a 4.3m (14ft) block of red sandstone, still stands. The stones formed an oval. In the centre was a cist (stone box) holding an urn containing fragments of burnt bone.

Giant's Grave, Arran

With views over Whiting Bay and Holy Island, the so-called Giant's Graves are two Neolithic chambered tombs. The stones of Giant's Grave North (pictured) are the remains of a chamber 6m (20ft) long and 1m (3.3ft) wide. In 1902, excavations discovered pottery shards, flint knives and leaf-shaped arrowheads here. Giant's Grave South, 40m (130ft) away, was part of the same burial complex.

Lochranza Castle, Arran

The majority of Lochranza Castle is 16th century, but the L-shaped tower house incorporates a hall-house dating back to the 13th century. The original hall-house, probably built by Dougall MacSween, Lord of Knapdale, was two storeys high, with the lord's lodging on the upper floor and the main door high in the seaward wall, reached by a removable wooden stair or ladder. When the building was converted to a tower house, the entrance was moved to the land-facing wall at ground level.

ABOVE:

Millport Bay, Great Cumbrae

Great Cumbrae, on the Firth of Clyde, has long been a popular daytrip and holiday destination for Glaswegians. The island's Gaelic name, Cumaradh, means 'place of the Cumbric people', referring to the Cumbric-speaking inhabitants of the Kingdom of Strathclyde, which ruled southern Scotland and northern England in the post-Roman period. Cumbric was a Brittonic language, closely related to Old Welsh.

RIGHT:

Millport, Great Cumbrae

Millport is Great Cumbrae's largest town, covering most of the small island's south coast. The town boasts the world's narrowest house, named the Wedge, which with a frontage of 1.19m (47in) barely has room for a front door. Located on Stuart Street just off the harbour front, its widest point is 3.35m (11ft). Other draws here include the smallest cathedral in Great Britain, completed in 1851 and seating just 100 people.

LEFT:

**Bruichladdich
Distillery, Islay**

Malt whisky distilling is
the island of Islay's second
largest employer, after
farming. Whiskies distilled
in the north of the island,
including Bruichladdich, have
a slightly lighter flavour than
the intensely peaty whiskies of
the south. The Bruichladdich
Distillery was first opened in
1881, but is not the island's
oldest legal distillery, which
is Bowmore, dating to 1779.
Bruichladdich copper pot stills
(pictured) are pear-shaped and
very tall.

TOP RIGHT:

**Bunnahabhain
Distillery, Islay**

Bunnahabhain, on the
northeast coast of Islay, is
one of eight distilleries on the
island. At one time, 23 legal
distilleries were in operation.
Islay's abundance of peat
is part of the success of its
whisky industry. The peat
is burned in kilns to dry the
malted barley used in the
distillation process.

LEFT:

Bunnahabhain village, Islay

The southernmost of the Inner Hebrides, Islay has been inhabited since the Mesolithic period. The oldest evidence of human habitation in Scotland was found on Islay, a flint arrowhead dated to 10,800 BC. By the Iron Age, Islay's inhabitants were constructing forts, such as the one at Dun Nosebridge. The village of Bunnahabhain was established in 1881 to house distillery workers.

ABOVE:

Lagavulin Distillery, Islay

The Lagavulin Distillery was officially opened in 1816, but there are records of illegal distilleries on the site since 1742. The history of whisky distilling on the island is far longer, with the skills probably brought to Islay by Irish monks in the Middle Ages. Like nearly all the Islay distilleries, Lagavulin is on the coast, with the sea air said to contribute to the flavour bestowed by the peat.

Oronsay Priory, Oronsay

The tidal island of Oronsay, in the Inner Hebrides, is linked to Colonsay by a causeway at low tide. The island has a population of eight, living in the farmhouse by Oronsay Priory. The 14th-century priory is dedicated to St Columba, the 6th-century Irish abbot who spread Christianity to Scotland. The priory is known for its distinctive carved crosses, the oldest of which, known as the Little Cross, is pictured.

Kiloran Beach, Colonsay

The oldest evidence of human habitation on Colonsay has been dated to 7000 BC, when the island's inhabitants filled a large pit with hundreds of thousands of burned hazelnut shells. Today, Colonsay has a permanent population of around 120, with many more visitors in summer, drawn by the peaceful beaches, wild goats and varied birdlife. The island is owned by the current Baron Strathcona and Mount Royal.

Seil, Slate Islands
The most northerly of the Slate Islands, Seil is connected to the mainland by the Clachan Bridge over the narrow Clachan Sound. The islands are named for their slate quarries, which were active from the 17th to the mid-20th century. Between Seil and the next island, Easdale, there was once another island, named Eilean-a-beithich. The island was quarried to 76m (249ft) below sea level, leaving only the outer rim, which gave way after a severe gale in 1881.

LEFT:

Baile Mòr, Iona

Baile Mòr is Iona's main settlement and home to many of its 170 permanent residents, who fish, croft and look after the 130,000 annual visitors. Iona, which is about 2 km (1.2 miles) off the southwest coast of Mull, was inhabited by fellow Gaels when Columba and 12 companions arrived in a coracle from Ireland in AD 563. The island, known as Hy, was ruled by the Gaelic kingdom of Dál Riata, which covered western Scotland and northeastern Ireland.

ABOVE AND RIGHT:

Iona Abbey, Iona

Little survives of St Columba's 6th-century monastery, which was damaged by Viking attacks. In 1200, Ragnall, Lord of the Isles, built the abbey here. It fell into ruin after the Scottish Reformation and was heavily restored in the 20th century. Forty-eight Scottish, eight Norwegian and four Irish kings were interred in the burial ground, as well as former British Labour Party leader John Smith, with the epitaph 'An honest man's the noblest work of God'.

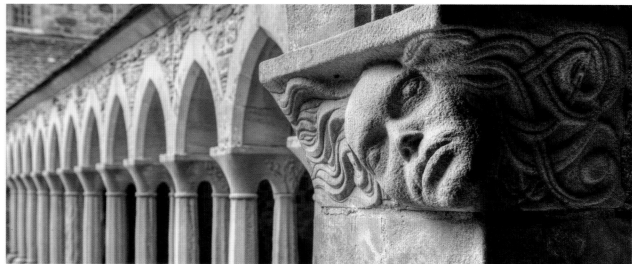

Staffa

The tiny island of Staffa lies about 10 km (6 miles) west of Mull. Its name comes from the Norse for 'pillar', thanks to its basalt columns. These were formed around 55–58 million years ago, after an eruption from the same volcanic fissure that formed the Giant's Causeway of Northern Ireland. As the thick flow of lava cooled, it shrank and cracked, forming regular-shaped columns, most of them hexagonal but ranging from three-sided to eight-sided. The most famous feature of the island is Fingal's Cave (pictured right), named after the mythical Irish and Scottish hero Fionn (or Fingal) mac Cumhaill. Legend has it that the Giant's Causeway and Staffa were once linked by a stone pavement, built by Fionn so he could fight the Scottish giant Benandonner.

ABOVE:

Mishnish Hotel and Pub, Tobermory, Mull

The 'Mish', as it is known to locals, is on the harbour front near the pier, in Tobermory, the capital of Mull. Serving since 1869, the Mish plays host to regular folk bands, as well as the Mull Music Festival. Held every April in various Tobermory venues, the festival features cèilidhs (from the Gaelic for 'visits') as well as fiddle, accordion and folk-rock bands.

RIGHT:

Tobermory, Mull

With a population of around 1000, Tobermory was built by the British Fisheries Society in 1788 to a design by Scottish engineer Thomas Telford. Legend tells us that a wrecked Spanish galleon, laden with gold, has lain at the bottom of Tobermory Bay since 1588. The sinking was the work of local witch Dòideag, who may also have been responsible for the unfortunate end of the entire Spanish Armada.

Duart Castle, Mull
This 13th-century castle was built by Clan MacDougall, but became the seat of Clan MacLean in the 14th century. After being surrendered to the Dukes of Argyll in 1691, the castle was largely dismantled. However, in 1911, the ruin was bought by the 26th Chief of the Clan MacLean, Sir Fitzroy Donald MacLean, and rebuilt.

LEFT:

Laig Bay, Eigg, Small Isles
Just 9km (5.6 miles) long and
5km (3 miles) wide, the island
of Eigg has been inhabited
since the Neolithic period.
The Irish priest St Donnán
of Eigg brought Christianity
to the island, building a
monastery here. In 617, he
and more than 50 others in his
community were martyred in
the monastery by bandits who
were possibly in the pay of a
pagan Pictish queen.

RIGHT:

Port Mòr, Muck, Small Isles
The smallest of the Small
Isles, Muck had a population
of 27 at the 2011 census.
Most live around the harbour
at Port Mòr. The island's
name comes from the Gaelic
'*mouach*', meaning 'swine',
referring to the many
porpoises in surrounding
waters, which were 'sea
swine'. The name has caused
some embarrassment to the
island's lairds, one of whom
tried to convince the visiting
Samuel Johnson and James
Boswell it was really called the
'Isle of Monk'.

Sligachan Bridge, Skye
Many visitors come to Skye to climb the steep Cuillin mountains, which rise to 992m (3255ft) at Sgùrr Alasdair. There are many possible etymologies for the name Cuillin, from the Old Norse '*kjöllen*', meaning the keel of a Viking longship, to a link to Cú Chulainn, the hero of Scots and Irish mythology, who learned his archery skills here from the Isle of Skye warrior woman Scáthach.

LEFT:

The Cleat, Skye
Taken from the slopes of the Quiraing, on Skye's Trotternish Peninsula, this photograph shows the Cleat hill, with Loch Cleat at its feet. The Quiraing is known for its dramatic rock formations, created by a series of massive landslips.

RIGHT:

Old Man of Storr, Skye
Situated on the Trotternish Peninsula, the hill of Storr rises to 719m (2359ft). On its slopes, the Old Man is one of many rock pinnacles in the vicinity, remnants left behind by the area's landslips. The slips were a result of the weight of 300-m (980-ft) thick lava flows on top of weaker sedimentary rocks. The sedimentary rocks split along faults, sending giant blocks sliding seawards.

LEFT:

Mealt Falls and Kilt Rock, Skye

On the northeast coast of the Trotternish Peninsula is the 90m (295ft) Mealt Falls. When the wind is strong, the water from Mealt Loch is blown away before it has a chance to crash into the Sound of Raasay below. A little further along the coast, the cliffs of Kilt Rock are so named because of their likeness to a kilt, with pleats formed by columns of basalt and a horizontal weave of sandstone at their base.

RIGHT:

Neist Point, Skye

The lighthouse at Neist Point was designed in 1909 by David Alan Stevenson of the prolific family of Scottish lighthouse designers. Today the light is operated remotely from Edinburgh. In the summer months, minke whales, common dolphins, harbour porpoises and basking sharks can be seen offshore.

Portree, Skye

Skye's largest town, Portree was a common departure point for those attempting to escape poverty by sailing for the Americas during the 18th and 19th centuries. The town's name is said to come from the Gaelic '*port righ*', meaning 'king's port', because of a visit by King James V in 1540. However, the name predates the visit, which suggests that it may come instead from '*port ruighe*', meaning 'port on a slope'.

BELOW:
Baleshare

A tidal island off the west coast of North Uist, in the Outer Hebrides, Baleshare's 60-strong population has benefitted from a permanent 350-m (1150-ft) long causeway, built in 1962. The 9sq km (3.5sq mile) island is remarkably flat and known for its long, sandy beach, which is threatened by coastal erosion.

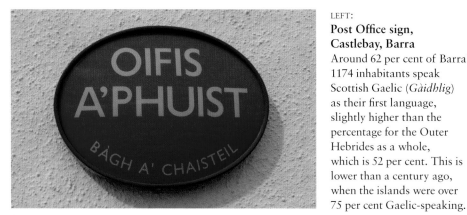

LEFT:
Post Office sign, Castlebay, Barra

Around 62 per cent of Barra's 1174 inhabitants speak Scottish Gaelic (*Gàidhlig*) as their first language, slightly higher than the percentage for the Outer Hebrides as a whole, which is 52 per cent. This is lower than a century ago, when the islands were over 75 per cent Gaelic-speaking.

RIGHT:
Kisimul Castle, Barra

The seat of Clan MacNeil since the late 15th century, Kisimul (from the Gaelic '*ciosamul*', meaning 'castle island') is accessible only by boat. In 2001, Iain MacNeil, the chief of Clan MacNeil, generously leased the castle to Historic Scotland for 1000 years in return for an annual payment of £1 and a bottle of whisky.

LEFT:

Eriskay

In the last century, Eriskay's population shrank as people searched for less tough work than crofting and fishing. However, the population grew from 133 in 2001 to 143 in 2011. Compton Mackenzie's 1947 novel *Whisky Galore* was based on the events here of 1941, when the SS *Politician* struck rocks offshore, carrying 264,000 bottles of Scotch whisky. After rescuing the crew, the islanders rescued the whisky. Some of those bottles are on display in Eriskay's only pub, the Politician.

TOP RIGHT:

South Uist

In 1851, half the population of South Uist was evicted by the landowner, John Gordon, who threw them onto waiting ships to make room for sheep-farming. In 2006, local residents bought the island, as well as Benbecula and Eriskay, from the then owner in the largest community buyout in Scottish history.

BOTTOM RIGHT:

Cleits, St Kilda

The St Kilda archipelago, the westernmost in the Hebrides, is known for its unique *cleits*, huts where food was preserved by wind rather than salting or smoking. Since 1930, when the remaining population of 36 was taken to the mainland at their own request, there has been no permanent population on St Kilda.

LEFT:

Summit view from Clisham, Harris, Lewis and Harris

At 799m (2,621ft), the Clisham is the highest mountain on Harris and the highest in the Outer Hebrides. Harris, though often referred to as an isle in its own right, is the more southerly and mountainous part of the island of Lewis and Harris. With an area of 2178sq km (841sq miles), this is the largest island in Scotland and the third largest in the British Isles, after Great Britain and Ireland.

RIGHT:

Callanish Stones, Lewis, Lewis and Harris

This circle of standing stones, surrounded by a cruciform arrangement, dates to between 2900 and 2600 BC. A chambered tomb within the circle was found to contain shards of pottery, some not in the local Hebridean style. This area on the west coast of Lewis must have been a focus for ritual activity for many centuries, as three other stone circles plus several arcs and single stones are found within a few kilometres.

ABOVE:

ABOVE:

Skara Brae, Mainland, Orkney

Europe's most complete Neolithic village, these eight homes were inhabited between around 3180 and 2500 BC. The stone-built houses were dug into mounds of old domestic waste, which gave much needed insulation. Each house had a large square living room with a stone hearth for heating and cooking, along with stone beds, cupboards, seats and storage boxes. The front door was a stone slab that could be closed by a bar that slid into holes in the door jambs. The village shared a drainage system, with a simple toilet in each home.

TOP LEFT:

Highland Park Distillery, Kirkwall, Mainland, Orkney

The most northerly distillery in Scotland, Highland Park produces its single malt with barley malted using a mixture of local peat and heather as fuel. The town of Kirkwall, with a population of 10,000, is Scotland's largest island settlement. Its name comes from the Norse '*kirkjuvagr*' ('church bay'). The Orkney Islands were invaded and annexed by Norway in 875, then annexed by Scotland in 1472 after Christian I of Norway defaulted on paying his daughter Margaret's dowry when she married James III of Scotland.

BOTTOM LEFT:

Auskerry Lighthouse, Auskerry, Orkney

Auskerry, in the eastern Orkneys, was uninhabited for 20 years after the automation of the lighthouse in the 1960s. Today the island is home to a family of four who keep a flock of rare North Ronaldsay sheep, which feed mainly on seaweed.

RIGHT:

St Margaret's Hope, South Ronaldsay, Orkney

The main town on South Ronaldsay is St Margaret's Hope, which may get its name from the Norwegian princess Margaret, granddaughter and heir of the Scottish King Alexander III, who died in Orkney aged seven in 1290.

LEFT:

Bressay, Shetland

Lying 168 km (104 miles) north of the Scottish mainland, the Shetland Islands were, like Orkney, annexed by Scotland from Norway in 1472. Of the roughly 100 islands in the archipelago, only 16 are inhabited, including the Mainland, with a population of 18,765, and Bressay, to the east, with 368 inhabitants. The lighthouse was built by Thomas and David Stevenson in 1858.

RIGHT:

Hermaness National Nature Reserve, Unst, Shetland

This rugged headland on the most northerly of the inhabited Shetland Islands, and the most northerly inhabited point of Great Britain, is home to colonies of puffins, great skuas, shags, gannets, guillemots and fulmars. Legend has it that the headland was once home to a friendly giant named Herman, who fought with a warlike giant named Saxe. After a terrible confrontation, they were both turned into rocks and turf by a local witch.

ABOVE:

Atlantic puffins, Isle of May National Nature Reserve
The isle of May, off Scotland's east coast in the Firth of Forth, is managed by Scottish Natural Heritage, to protect its harbour and grey seals, as well as the 285 bird species that have been recorded there, including the Atlantic puffin.

LEFT:

Harbour seal, South Uist
Two species of seals can be found in Scottish waters, the harbour seal and grey seal. About 24,000 harbour seals and 135,000 grey seals live around Scottish coasts. Harbour seals prefer sheltered waters, being more often found on the east coast of Outer Hebridean islands such as South Uist than the west. Adult male harbour seals measure around 1.45m (4ft 9 in) long.

RIGHT:

White-tailed eagle, Skye
The white-tailed eagle became extinct in the United Kingdom in the early 20th century. Reintroduction programmes have established breeding pairs on the islands of Skye, Rum and Mull and along the west coast of the mainland. With a wingspan up to 2.45m (8ft), the white-tailed eagle is the United Kindom's largest bird of prey. The diet of these eagles consists primarily of fish and seabirds.

Glasgow: Dear Green Place

Glasgow's nickname, 'Dear Green Place', comes from a translation of its old Cumbric name, Glas Gau ('green hollow'). The nickname is less ironic than many of its users may intend, since despite its industrial heritage, Scotland's most populous city has more than 90 parks, making it one of Europe's greenest cities. The city grew from settlements beside the River Clyde that, by the 6th century, clustered around the church of St Mungo, on the site of today's Glasgow Cathedral. During the 18th century, Glasgow's merchants made their fortunes from trade with the Americas, particularly in tobacco. In the 19th century, there were few cities that could compete with Glasgow's industries, with a prodigious output in shipbuilding, textiles, chemicals and much more.

It was during this period of growth and immense wealth that many of Glasgow's most impressive projects were undertaken, from the splendid City Chambers to the Kelvingrove Museum. Yet, at the same time, much of the city's working population lived in overcrowded and unsanitary tenements. The first half of the 20th century saw significant urban decline and deprivation, but from the mid-1950s successive waves of urban planners, along with hard-working inhabitants from entrepreneurs to artists, have overseen the city's regeneration as one of Europe's most culturally innovative cities. New life has been breathed into deserted shipyards, while there is no end to the iconic and daring new building projects, from squiggly bridges to armadillo-shaped auditoriums.

OPPOSITE:
River Clyde
Glasgow boasts 21 bridges over the River Clyde, which was dredged from 1768 to allow large ocean-going ships to travel all the way into the city. In this photograph taken from Glasgow Tower, the bridges (from front to back) are the 2002 pedestrian Millennium Bridge, the 1998 pedestrian Bell's Bridge, the 2006 road Clyde Arc and the 1970 road Kingston Bridge.

ABOVE:

Tradeston Bridge, River Clyde

This S-shaped bridge for pedestrians and cyclists is known locally as the Squiggly Bridge. It was completed in 2009 to link the south bank district of Tradeston with the International Financial Services District on the north side of the river. The aim of the iconic new construction was to regenerate the Tradeston riverfront, a former industrial zone, kickstarting new office and housing developments.

RIGHT:

Clyde Arc, River Clyde

This 2006 road, pedestrian and cycle bridge is known to Glaswegians as the Squinty Bridge because it crosses the River Clyde diagonally. Only newcomers to the city refer to the structure by its official name. Like the nearby Squiggly Bridge, this construction was part of a major plan to regenerate riverside areas. The bridge's 96-m (315-ft) main span features a steel bowstring asymmetric arch.

LEFT:

**SEC Armadillo
and SSE Hydro,
Scottish Event Campus**
Originally named the Clyde
Auditorium, the Armadillo
had been renamed by locals
even before completion in
2000. The design by Foster &
Partners was inspired not by
the armoured mammal but
by the Clyde's shipbuilding
heritage, its shells representing
ships' hulls. The Hydro venue
is more prosaically named
after the former Scottish
Hydro energy supplier.

RIGHT:

**Glasgow Tower,
Glasgow Science Centre**
Completed in 2001, this
observation tower holds
the record for being the
world's tallest fully rotating
freestanding structure. The
127m (417ft) tower can
turn a full 360 degrees. The
landmark is in the shape of an
aircraft wing. When needed, it
has motors to turn it into the
wind to improve stability.

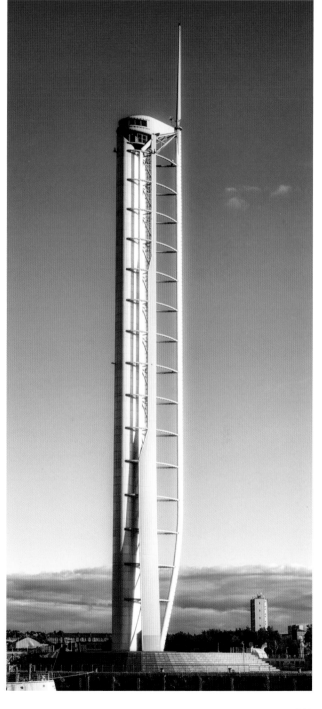

The *Glenlee* and Riverside Museum, Pointhouse Quay
Built in Port Glasgow in 1896, the *Glenlee* started life as a cargo
ship. Shipbuilding at Port Glasgow, 28 km (17 miles) down
the Clyde from the city centre, began in 1762, before dredging
of the river allowed the industry to take root in the city itself.
The Riverside Museum, home of the Glasgow Museum of
Transport, was built on the site of the A & J Inglis shipyard,
which operated from 1862 to 1962. The 2011 museum was
designed by Iraqi-British architect Zaha Hadid.

Finnieston Crane

This immense cantilever crane, with a lifting capacity of 175 tonnes (193 tons), is 53m (174ft) tall with a 46-m (152-ft) cantilever jib. Since 1988, the crane has not been in working order, but has been maintained as a symbol of the city's industrial heritage. From 1932, the crane lifted heavy machinery, including 30,000 locomotives, onto ships for export across the world. Only 11 giant cantilever cranes are still in existence, including four on the River Clyde.

LEFT:

McLennan Arch, Glasgow Green

No one has been able to decide where to put the McLennan Arch since it was first constructed in 1796 by Neoclassical architects James and Robert Adam as part of the facade of the city Assembly Rooms. After the building was demolished in 1890, the arch was reconstructed in 1892 on Monteith Row, at the expense of James McLennan, then moved in 1922 to the west edge of the Green, before moving in 1991 to its present position.

BELOW:

South Portland Street Suspension Bridge

This footbridge is an extension of South Portland Street in Laurieston, on the south side of the Clyde, linking it with the city centre on the north side. The 1853 wrought-iron bridge, with sandstone arches at either end, has a suspension span of 126m (414ft). Facing the river on the south side is Carlton Place (pictured), with terraces dating from around 1802, intended as a showpiece for the suburb built by John and David Laurie.

Statues, George Square

Glasgow's principal city square was developed between 1787 and the 1820s, while the surrounding area was laid out on a rationalist grid plan. The square was named after King George III (1738–1820) and a statue of the king was intended to grace the square's centre, but British defeat in the American War of Independence in 1783, costing the city's tobacco lords their fortunes with the loss of their plantations, caused a rethink. A cenotaph, plus twelve statues to notable people, ornament the square, including (from left to right) a rare equestrian statue of Queen Victoria (1854), Scottish member of parliament James Oswald (1856) and Robert Burns (1877), regarded as the national poet of Scotland.

Glasgow City Chambers, George Square

Home to Glasgow City Council, the City Chambers were constructed between 1882 and 1888 to a design by Scottish architect William Young, who won a competition to garner the commission. The interior features a dramatic staircase carved from Carrara marble, alabaster wall panels and ceilings decorated with gold leaf. The staircase was seen in the 2000 film *The House of Mirth*, starring Gillian Anderson.

Entrance to Glasgow City Chambers

There is little doubt that it was the grandiosity of William Young's designs that impressed the city fathers, who were keen to demonstrate 19th-century Glasgow's great wealth and industry. The building's exterior is in ornate Beaux-Arts style. While drawing on French Neoclassicism, the style incorporated more florid Baroque and Rococo elements in its decoration and signature wealth of statuary.

Exterior of Glasgow City Chambers

The original budget for the building was £150,000, but the designs and the costs soared skyward, finally reaching £578,232, equivalent to around £70 million today. When the building was opened by Queen Victoria in 1888, it was the first large public building in the United Kingdom to have electric lighting throughout. The original 'electroliers' in the Banqueting Hall are still in working order.

Ashton Lane, West End
Cobbled Ashton Lane, close to the University of Glasgow, is known for its restaurants and bars. One of the most famous businesses is the Ubiquitous Chip, so named as, when it started trading in 1971, it was almost the only restaurant in Glasgow not to have chips on the menu. Also here is the Grosvenor Picture Theatre, which first opened in 1921.

Barrowland Ballroom, East End
This venue was built by local trader Maggie McIver, who founded the nearby Barras street market, in operation since 1921. 'Barras' means 'barrow' in Glaswegian dialect. The Ballroom, opened in 1934, has street-level halls for weekend markets, plus a first-floor dance hall which has hosted bands from the Foo Fighters to U2. The facade is decorated with an animated neon sign that may be the largest of its kind in the United Kingdom.

Princes Square, Buchanan Street

This shopping centre is based around a merchants' premises designed in 1841 by the Neoclassical Glaswegian architect John Baird. In 1986, the existing sandstone building and cobbled square were enclosed by a glass domed and vaulted roof, with new galleries and stairs giving access to the upper storeys. The old cellars were excavated for extra shopping space. In 2016, the centre's striking interplay of old and new led to its being named Scotland's best building of the last 100 years in a public poll for the Festival of Architecture.

CENTRAL S

Central Station

Scotland's busiest train station opened in 1879, but soon reached capacity and was rebuilt in 1901–05. The most famous feature of the station building is the glass-walled bridge that carries the platforms over Argyll Street (pictured). It is nicknamed the Hielanman's Umbrella ('Highlandman's Umbrella'), which, like all nicknames for landmarks in the city, has stuck. The name comes from the Highlanders who, having come to the city for work, gathered under the bridge to exchange news and shelter from the rain.

Buchanan Street

Glasgow's premier shopping
street, Buchanan Street is the
sixth most expensive street
for retail rents in the United
Kingdom, topped only by five
streets in London. The street
is named after its 18th-century
developers, the Buchanans of
Drumpellier, who lost their
tobacco fortune after the
American Revolution. Many
fine 19th-century buildings
remain, including the 1808
St George's Tron Church.

**Hutcheson Street
and Hutchesons' Hall**

Hutchesons' Hall was
constructed in 1802–05
as Hutchesons' Hospital,
to designs by Glaswegian
architect David Hamilton.
It replaced a 1641 hospital,
paid for by a bequest from
the local Hutcheson brothers.
Having fallen into disrepair,
the refurbished building
is today occupied by
a restaurant.

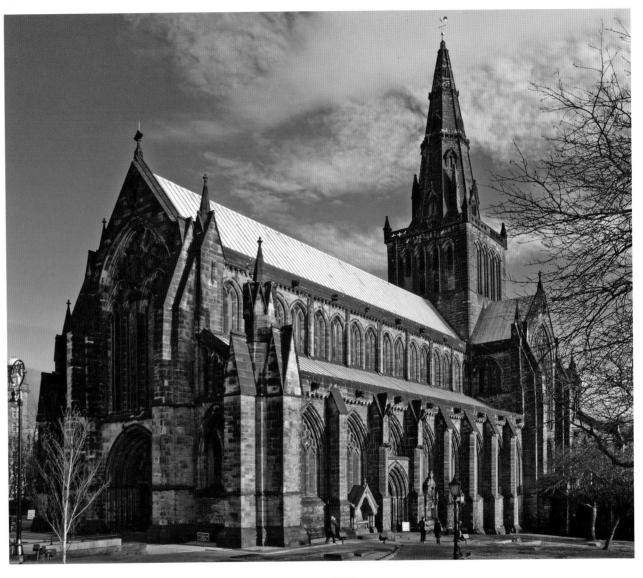

LEFT:

Interior, Glasgow Cathedral

The Gothic cathedral, also known as St Mungo's, was consecrated in 1197, making it Glasgow's oldest building. The tomb of St Mungo is in the 13th-century crypt. In the 6th century, Mungo built a church here and worked to convert the local Picts to Christianity. The community that collected around him is said to have grown into Glasgow, although there were already settlements in the area. St Mungo died here in 613.

ABOVE:

Glasgow Cathedral, Cathedral Square

The cathedral we see today was mostly built during the 13th to 15th centuries, although the oldest parts of the building date to 1174–99. It is the only cathedral on the Scottish mainland to have survived the Reformation almost intact, thanks to the affection the people of Glasgow felt for the building. The 15th-century spire, not to mention the green copper-covered roof, acts as a landmark for miles around.

161

East Quadrangle, Main Building, University of Glasgow
Founded in 1451, the University of Glasgow is the fourth-oldest university in the United Kingdom, after Oxford, Cambridge and St Andrews. Since 1870, when it moved from a cramped site on the High Street, the university has been based at Gilmorehill in the city's West End. The main building was designed in Gothic Revival style by English architect Sir George Gilbert Scott, who died in 1878 before completion. His son John Oldrid Scott finished the twin quadrangles and Bute Hall (pictured to the right). The local pale sandstone cladding and romantically turreted exterior hide a cutting-edge Victorian construction, with an internal riveted iron frame.

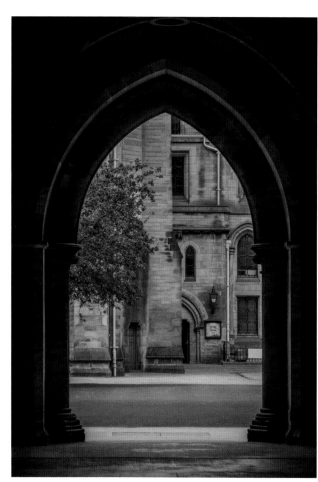

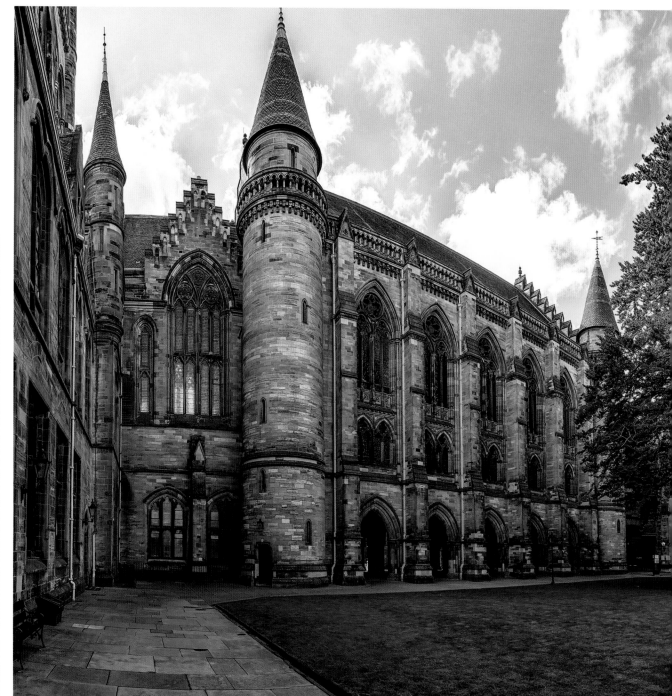

**The Cloisters,
Glasgow University**
The Cloisters connect the
West and East Quadrangles
(see previous page) of
Glasgow University's main
building. The fluted columns
support ribbed vaulting, with
masonry piping where the
vaults intersect. This complex
technique was groundbreaking
in the late 11th century and
picked up enthusiastically
during the Gothic Revival.

LEFT:
House for an Art Lover, Bellahouston Park
On Glasgow's south side, in Bellahouston Park, is one of Glaswegian architect, designer and artist Charles Rennie Mackintosh's (1868–1928) most elegant visions. The art venue was completed in 1996 to 1901 designs by Mackintosh and his wife, the painter and glass artist Margaret Macdonald (1864–1933). Mackintosh and Macdonald were founding figures of the Glasgow School and the celebrated Glasgow Style.

BELOW:
The Willow Tea Rooms
The original 1903 Willow Tea Rooms were designed in their entirety by Mackintosh. He remodelled the exterior of the 1860s tenement block and oversaw the interior decorative elements, right down to the design of the cutlery and the uniform of the staff. The Tea Rooms at 217 Sauchiehall Street reopened in July 2018 after a four year restoration to return them to their former glory, they are now known as 'Mackintosh at the Willow'.

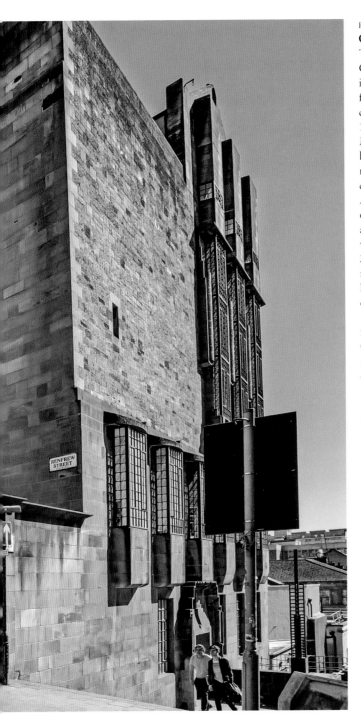

FAR LEFT AND LEFT:

Glasgow School of Art
The most famous work by
Charles Rennie Mackintosh
is without doubt his building
for Glasgow School of Art,
completed between 1896 and
1909. The building shows
Mackintosh's interplay
between strong, sturdy
rectilinear forms and more
delicate curves. The School of
Art is regularly named as one
of the United Kingdom's finest
and best-loved buildings. It
was badly damaged by fire in
2014 and again in 2018, during
restoration works. It is widely
hoped that the masterpiece
can be saved.

RIGHT:

Queen's Cross Church
Mackintosh's only church
design to be completed,
Queen's Cross opened in
1899. Overall, the church
draws on an almost Norman
simplicity, but with an airier
Art Nouveau and even
Gothic styling in its windows
and pulpit. The church,
now decommissioned, is
home to the Charles Rennie
Mackintosh Society.

BELOW:

Kelvingrove Art Gallery and Museum
Financed by the profits from the 1888 Glasgow International
Exhibition and opened for the 1901 International Exhibition
(the first and second of four International Exhibitions held in
the city), this museum was designed by Sir John W. Simpson and
E.J. Milner Allen in elaborately ornamented Baroque Revival
style. The Spitfire LA198 served with the 602 (City of Glasgow)
Royal Air Force Squadron between 1947 and 1949.

RIGHT:

Gallery of Modern Art
Opened in 1996, the GoMA hosts works by Scottish artists such
as John Bellany and Ken Currie, as well as international artists
including David Hockney and Andy Warhol. The building
started life in 1778 as the home of William Cunninghame, who
made his fortune through the devastating triangular trade of
slaves and tobacco. The Corinthian pillars were added in 1832
by David Hamilton, when the building was the Royal Exchange.

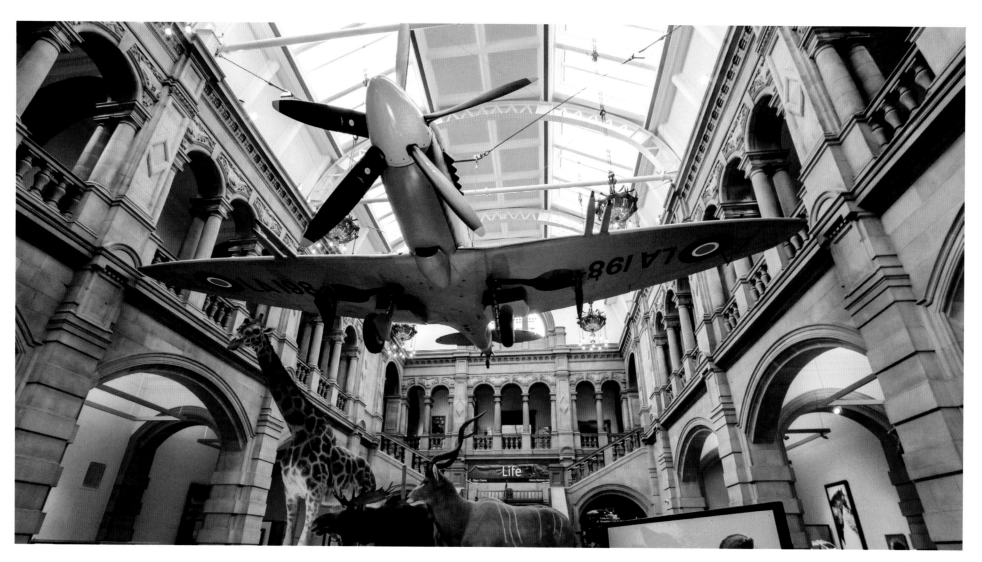

LEFT:

Pollok House, Pollok Country Park

Located in the southern outskirts of Glasgow, Pollok House was home to the Stirling Maxwell family until 1966, when it was gifted to the City of Glasgow. The fine country house was completed in 1752, with some involvement by the Neoclassical architect William Adam. The discussions for the founding of the National Trust for Scotland took place at Pollok.

BELOW:

Knot Garden, Pollok House

The gardens at Pollok are renowned for hosting 1000 varieties of rhododendrons and a beech tree that may be 250 years old, with a trunk that reaches an extraordinary width of 10m (33ft). A castle was first erected around this spot by the Stirling Maxwells in the 13th century, with a second castle built in the 15th century near the current stable block.

LEFT:

People's Palace and Winter Gardens, Glasgow Green

This museum and glasshouse were opened in 1898, offering reading and recreation rooms, exhibits, a gallery and a collection of exotic plants. The Palace was intended to provide respite for local people from Glasgow's overcrowded East End. Outside the museum is a plaque to 'Sister' Smudge (*c*.1970–2000), the museum's rodent-catcher who gained membership of the General, Municipal and Boilermakers (GMB) Union in the 1980s.

LEFT:

White Cart Water, Linn Park

Where it flows through Linn Park, in Glasgow's southern suburbs, the River Cart is known as White Cart Water. The River Cart is mentioned in a Robert Burns (1759–96) poem called 'The Gallant Weaver': 'Where Cart rins rowin to the sea, By mony a flow'r and spreading tree, There lives a lad, the lad for me, He is a gallant weaver.' The park, acquired by the city in 1919, takes its name from this waterfall, as '*linn*' means waterfall in Old Scottish.

BELOW:

Ha'penny Bridge, Linn Park

Built some time between 1811 and 1820, the Ha'penny Bridge is a very early example of a single-span cast-iron bridge in Scotland. The bridge's elliptical arch and decorative pierced ironwork suited it to its picturesque parkland setting. The bridge gets its name from the coin-shaped piercings in the arch. It is not known which engineer or foundry constructed the work, but they were clearly highly skilled.

Glasgow Necropolis

The Glasgow Necropolis opened in 1833, since which time an estimated 50,000 people have been buried here, although only 3500 of them have dedicated monuments. Overlooking Glasgow's East End, a seated angel (pictured left) memorializes the Whitelaw family. On her pediment are words from Corinthians: 'We shall all be changed in a moment, in the twinkling of an eye, at the last trump.' The twin tower blocks, which were for a while the tallest buildings in Scotland, were demolished shortly after this photograph was taken.

Villages, Towns and Burghs: Industry and Innovation

In Scotland, as in the rest of the United Kingdom, city status is granted by letters patent from the monarch of the United Kingdom. Today, there are seven cities in Scotland, from the largest to smallest: Glasgow, Edinburgh, Aberdeen, Dundee, Inverness, Perth and Stirling. Before the 1707 Acts of Union, the Scottish monarch granted the status or royal burgh to the largest and most important towns, the earliest of these charters given during the reign of David I (1124–1153), including to Linlithgow and Montrose. Before this period, Scotland did not have towns by today's standards, its largest settlements just clusters of houses and workshops around a monastery or castle, such as the village that grew up around the monastery that held the relics of St Andrew.

Today, Scotland's settlements include isolated farming communities and fishing villages that still rely on these age-old industries. At the other extreme, Scottish settlements also include the hard-working industrial towns and cities of the Central Belt, which stretches from Dundee in the east to Ayr in the west. Today, the monuments and museums of many of Scotland's settlements allow us to take an imaginative step back in time, whether into the heyday of Paisley's textile mills or into the medieval cloisters of the monasteries of the Borders. Yet Scottish towns and cities are also determined to march into the future through their reinvention and reinvigoration, drawing on the legends and industry of the past to create new monuments, from Falkirk's *Kelpies* to Dundee's design museum.

OPPOSITE:

Mercat Cross, Castlegate, Aberdeen
Since at least as long ago as the 12th century, mercat crosses have designated the place in Scottish towns where the monarch or local baron had granted the right to hold a market. There are 126 surviving examples in Scottish towns and cities. The mercat cross of Aberdeen, built in 1686, features a unicorn, symbol of the Scottish royal family, at the top of its central shaft.

Linlithgow Palace, Linlithgow, West Lothian
In 1542, Linlithgow Palace was the birthplace of Mary, Queen of Scots, although she was soon taken to the greater safety of Stirling Castle. There had been a royal manor house on the site of Linlithgow from the mid-12th century, during the reign of King David I. The current palace was largely built on the orders of King James I (1394–1437). The palace was burnt out in 1746 by an English army, after the Jacobite Rising.

LEFT AND BOTTOM LEFT:

Fort George, Inverness-shire
This star-shaped fort was built from 1748–69 to help pacify the Highlands following the Jacobite Rising of 1745. The famous family of Scottish architects, William, Robert, John and James Adams, oversaw construction. The garrison, still in use, is separated from the outer earthworks by a dry moat (pictured left). In 2016, Minister of Defence Michael Fallon announced that the barracks would close in 2032 because the Highland rebellions were over.

RIGHT:

River Ness, Inverness
The northernmost city in the United Kingdom, Inverness is situated at the mouth of the River Ness, which flows from Loch Ness. Taken from the tower of Inverness Castle, this photograph shows St Andrew's Cathedral, on the opposite bank. Its spires have unusual square tops, as funds for the cathedral's construction ran out in 1869, before they could be completed.

Stirling Castle, Stirling

No one is quite sure who said it first, but it is often quoted that 'He who holds Stirling, holds Scotland'. Situated at Scotland's geographical heart, Stirling is at the furthest downstream bridging point of the River Forth before it broadens into the Firth of Forth, making it a vital waypoint for travel north or south. This is why there has been a castle on Stirling's Castle Hill since at least 1110. The current castle dates from the 14th to early 18th centuries, during which time it suffered eight sieges. The mountain of Stùc a' Chroin ('Peak of Danger' in Scottish Gaelic) rises behind the city.

OPPOSITE:

Balvenie Castle, Dufftown, Moray

This ruined castle was built in the 12th century by the Comyn family, then passed to the powerful Earls of Douglas known as the Black Douglases, in the 14th century. In 1455, the Black Douglases were defeated by James II at the Battle of Arkinholm, at which point the castle was forfeited to the crown. The battle was a key step towards a strong, centralized monarchy.

ABOVE AND TOP RIGHT:

Glenfiddich Distillery, Dufftown

Glenfiddich (meaning 'valley of the deer' in Scottish Gaelic) is the bestselling Scotch single malt whisky. A single malt must be distilled at a single distillery using a pot still and a mash of malted barley. The distillery has 32 'swan neck' copper pot stills, smaller than those used by most distilleries but with a joint annual capacity of 13 million litres (3.4 million gallons).

BOTTOM RIGHT:

Statue of William and Elizabeth Grant, Glenfiddich Distillery

William Grant founded the Glenfiddich Distillery in 1886. As a young man, he had worked as a bookkeeper at the local Mortlach Distillery, finally saving enough money to open his own enterprise at the age of 47. The current owner of the business, Glenn Gordon, is William and his wife Elizabeth's great great grandson.

The Law, Dundee

This hill ('law' comes from the Anglo-Saxon '*hlaw*', meaning mound) in central Dundee was the site of an Iron Age hill fort, while graves dating to 1500 BC have been found on its slopes. The Law is the remains of a volcanic sill, formed when lava flowed through the side vent of a nearby volcano 400 million years ago. Slowly, glaciers, as well as wind and rain, wore away the softer overlying rock. At 174m (572ft) high, the Law offers great views over the city and to the Sidlaw Hills.

Statue of Desperate Dan and Dawg, High St, Dundee

The Wild West character of Desperate Dan made his first appearance in the first issue of *The Dandy*, on 4 December 1937. Dan, created by cartoonist Dudley D. Watkins, was regularly accompanied by his faithful pet Dawg. *The Dandy*, along with *The Beano*, was published by Dundee-based company D.C. Thomson. *The Dandy* reached its peak in the 1950s, when it was selling 2 million copies a week. Sadly, it closed in 2013.

McManus Galleries, Dundee

Opened in 1867 as the Albert Institute, as a memorial to Prince Albert, the McManus Galleries today hold exhibits on Dundee's history as well as fine and decorative arts. The core of the building was designed in Gothic Revival style by English architect George Gilbert Scott, also responsible for the main building of the University of Glasgow. The building has suffered from subsidence caused by the boggy ground beneath.

Victoria and Albert Museum, Dundee
This sister to London's Victoria and Albert Museum opened in 2018, hosting Scottish and global decorative arts, including interiors by Charles Rennie Mackintosh, Victorian glassware by Christopher Dresser and exhibits on shipbuilding. The monumental, shiplike building, clad in stacked concrete slabs, was designed by Japanese architect Kengo Kuma.

North Carr lightship, Victoria Dock, Dundee
Bought from a scrapyard for £1 in 2010, the *North Carr* is waiting in a dock on Dundee's River Tay for restoration as a floating museum. Built by A&J Inglis in Glasgow in 1932–3, the *North Carr* is the last surviving Scottish lightship. The vessel's job was to warn ships of the treacherous North Carr rocks, off Fife Ness, the most easterly point in Fife.

Harbour, Aberdeen
Until the 1970s, Aberdeen's key industries were textiles, shipbuilding and paper-making. The first major offshore oil find was in 1970, but Queen Elizabeth II did not press the button to start the flow of oil from the rigs to the refinery at Grangemouth until 1975. Since then, the oil industry has kept Aberdeen's seaport busy and the city one of the most prosperous in Scotland, despite a recent downturn. Many of Aberdeen's Victorian buildings, including the castellated Salvation Army Citadel (pictured at far right) are constructed from granite, earning it the nickname 'Granite City'.

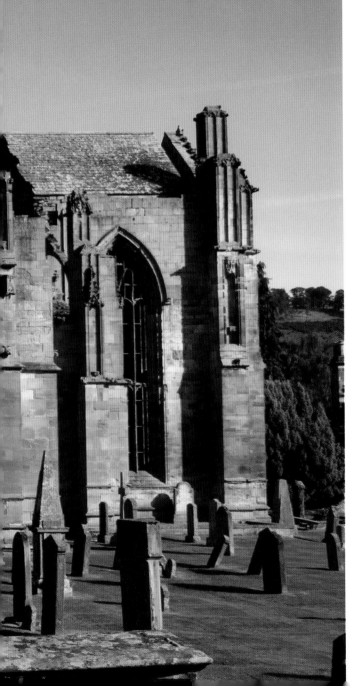

LEFT:

Melrose Abbey, Melrose, Scottish Borders

This largely ruined abbey was founded in 1136 by the Cistercians at the request of King David I. The Gothic abbey is decorated with carvings of gargoyles, dragons and saints. A lead container found below the Chapter House is believed to hold the embalmed heart of King Robert the Bruce (1274–1329), who successfully battled to regain Scotland's independence. The heart was reburied, then covered by a plinth.

BELOW:

Jedburgh Abbey, Jedburgh, Scottish Borders

Jedburgh Abbey was also established by King David I, in 1138. The Romanesque-Gothic abbey, home to the Augustinians, was intended to demonstrate David's power over the Borders region. In 1560, during the Scottish Reformation, the monks were allowed to stay at the site, but the abbey was turned into a parish church for the reformed religion. In 1871, the ruined structure was finally deemed unsafe for worship to continue.

197

New Bridge, Ayr, Ayrshire
Ayr's New Bridge over the
River Ayr was begun in
1786, which distinguishes it
from the Auld Bridge, which
probably dates back to 1470.
The New Bridge collapsed
and had to be rebuilt after
a severe storm in 1879. The
1786 Robert Burns poem
'The Brigs of Ayr' relates an
argument between the two
bridges. The New Bridge
calls the old one a 'sic an
ugly, Gothic hulk', while the
Auld Bridge retorts with a
prescient warning: 'Conceited
gowk! puff'd up wi' windy
pride! This mony a year I've
stood the flood an' tide; And
tho' wi' crazy eild I'm sair
forfairn, I'll be a brig when
ye're a shapeless cairn!'

St Matthew's Church, Perth, Perth and Kinross
A landmark in central Perth, St Matthew's towers over the River Tay. Local finds have shown that the site of Perth (from the Pictish for 'wood') has been inhabited for at least 8000 years. It has been known as the Fair City since the publication in 1828 of Sir Walter Scott's novel *The Fair Maid of Perth*, set in the Middle Ages and telling the loves and adventures of Catharine Glover, daughter of a glovemaker.

Anchor Mill, Paisley, Renfrewshire

By the 19th century, the town of Paisley was a centre of the Scottish weaving industry. Until the 1820s, when the Jacquard loom was introduced, weaving was a cottage industry. From then on, the process was mechanized in purpose-built mills. By 1850, there were more than 7000 weavers at work here. It was in Paisley that the expensive and delicate woollen Paisley shawls were created, featuring the Paisley pattern. This teardrop-shaped motif originated in Persia but was popularized by the town's weavers. The Anchor Mill, beside the River Cart, was built in 1886. The last of Paisley's mills closed in the 1990s.

New Lanark, Lanarkshire

This village was founded in 1786 by the entrepreneur and philanthropist David Dale, who built cotton mills and housing for their workers here, making use of the power provided by the River Clyde's falls. The mills operated until 1968. Today, the buildings have been restored and are listed as a UNESCO World Heritage Site.

Old Course, St Andrews Links, Fife

Formally established in 1552, the Old Course at St Andrews is one of the oldest golf courses in the world. The Royal and Ancient Golf Club of St Andrews club house is next to the first tee, but this is a public course on common land, so anyone can play without being a member of this or one of the Links' other clubs. Golf, in a form recognizable to us today, developed in 15th-century Scotland. The game was so popular in 1457 that James II felt forced to ban it as it was preventing young men from practising their archery.

LEFT:

**Undergraduates,
St Andrews, Fife**
It is tradition for the
students of the University
of St Andrews to take a
Sunday-morning walk
on the pier, wearing their
distinctive undergraduate
gowns. Founded in 1410–13,
St Andrews is the oldest
university in Scotland and
the third oldest in the United
Kingdom, after Oxford
and Cambridge.

RIGHT:

East Sands, St Andrews
In the mid-8th century, the
Pictish king Óengus I built
a monastery here to house
relics of St Andrew, who,
according to Christian
tradition, was born in 6 BC in
Galilee. Particularly following
the building of the cathedral
(pictured right, beside the
slightly older, square-shaped
St Rules tower) in 1158,
St Andrews became the most
important pilgrimage site in
Scotland. At 119m (390ft)
long the largest church built
in Scotland, the cathedral fell
into disuse after the Scottish
Reformation and its stones
were used by the townsfolk.

LEFT:

Crail, Fife

Possibly founded by the Picts, the village of Crail was made a royal burgh by King William the Lion in 1178. Burghs, which were given charters, were towns granted the right to have their own magistrates and councils and to conduct extensive trade. Each royal burgh had representation in the Scottish Parliament. The white customs house (pictured at the far right) dates from the 1690s.

ABOVE:

Lobster creels, Crail

In Scotland, lobster pots are known as creels. They are made of net stretched over a steel or plastic frame. Baited creels are dropped from a boat to the seabed, where they wait until they are retrieved. Creel fishing became widespread in the 19th century. Today, there are more than 1000 creel fishing boats in Scotland. One of many places to sample fresh lobster in Crail is the Lobster Hut (pictured) on the harbour.

St Monans, Fife
The village of St Monans is named after a saint about whom little is known for certain but who may have been a monk killed during a Viking raid in 875. It is possible that St Monan was a companion to St Adrian, who built monasteries on the Isle of May, off the coast of Fife. It is said that Monan set up a chapel on the site of the present village.

St Abbs, Berwickshire
The first fisherman's house was built here in the mid-18th century. Before that, the fishermen who launched their boats from the beach had to carry their creels more than 2 km (1.5 miles) from the village of Coldingham. It was not until the 1890s that a new name had been given to the settlement of 'Coldingham Shore'. St Aebbe was a noblewoman who founded a monastery nearby.

LEFT:

Chatelherault, Hamilton, South Lanarkshire

The name of this country park, centred on its elegant hunting lodge (pictured), comes from the French town of Châtellerault. James Hamilton, Earl of Arran, was granted the title Duc de Châtellerault in 1548 in gratitude for his help in arranging the marriage between Mary, Queen of Scots and Francis, later Francis II of France. The 1734 hunting lodge, which contained kennels, stables and accommodation, was designed by William Adam, who called it 'The Dogg Kennel'.

RIGHT:

Hamilton Mausoleum, Hamilton

This mausoleum was built by Alexander Hamilton, 10th Duke of Hamilton, in 1842–58 in the grounds of his country house, which has since been demolished. The Roman-style mausoleum, 37m (123ft) high, was the last resting place of the duke, in a genuine Egyptian sarcophagus, along with several family members. The structure has one of the longest echoes in any manmade structure: it takes 15 seconds for the sound of a slammed door to fade.

ABOVE:

Falkirk Wheel, Falkirk
This iconic rotating boat lift opened in 2002, raising boats by 24m (79ft) between the levels of the Forth and Clyde Canal and the higher Union Canal. The Union Canal is higher still than the aqueduct that meets the top of the wheel, so boats must still pass through two locks. To ride the wheel, boats manoeuvre inside the circular portions of the wheel's two arms, which hold gondolas that lift 500 tonnes (550 tons) of water and boat.

RIGHT:

The Kelpies, **The Helix, Falkirk**
These 30-m (100-ft) high equine statues, by Scottish artist Andy Scott, were constructed in 2013. The statues are the centrepiece of The Helix, a land transformation project that has created parkland and leisure spaces beside the new extension of the Forth and Clyde Canal. Kelpies are shape-shifting water spirits, sometimes taking the form of a horse. They aptly represent the transformative nature of the project.

LEFT:

Invergordon, Ross and Cromarty
Invergordon is a port on the Cromarty Firth, which has been
used for stacking oil rigs since the start of the North Sea
oil business in the 1970s. Some of the rigs are waiting for
maintenance work at the Invergordon Service Base, while some
are awaiting a tow to another destination, including scrapyards
in India and Bangladesh. Looking to the future, the area is also
investing in the manufacture of offshore wind turbines.

ABOVE:

Oil refinery, Grangemouth, Falkirk
In operation since 1924, Grangemouth is now Scotland's only
oil refinery. At the start, Grangemouth processed crude oil
imported from the Persian Gulf. Since 1975, crude oil has been
piped here from the North Sea oilfields via the Forties Pipeline.
Today, the plant produces petrol, diesel and jet fuel; liquefied
petroleum gas for domestic heating; and petrochemicals for use
in manufacturing plastics.

Inveraray, Argyll and Bute

On the shores of Loch Fyne, the former royal burgh of Inveraray has an unusual coat of arms. It features a net into which five herring are swimming, with the Latin motto '*Semper tibi pendeat halec*', meaning 'May the fish sauce always be yours', although the intended meaning may have been 'herring' rather than 'fish sauce'. The arms are testament to Loch Fyne's important herring fisheries.